Fever

Fever

poems

RON KOERTGE

RED HEN PRESS | Los Angeles, California

Fever

Cover image by Paul Williamson
Cover Design by Olga Vaynkof
Book design by Michael Vukadinovich

ISBN: 1-59709-016-6
ISBN-13: 978-1-59709-016-2
Library of Congress Catalog Card Number: 2004118134

Published by Red Hen Press

The City of Los Angeles Department of Cultural Affairs, Los Angeles County Arts Commission and National Endowment for the Arts partially support Red Hen Press.

First edition

Acknowledgements

Cider Press Review: "Amaryllis Rescue," "American Wife," "Found"; *Court Green*: "Blue"; 5 A.M.: "Where I Live," "Reading the School Literary Magazine," "Flying to Nevada with Ten Thousand Dollars in My Sock," "Heaven's Just Like Here Only Everything's Clouds"; *Free Lunch*: "Smoke"; *Jacket*: "Seven Brides For Seven Brothers, "Consolations of Cinema"; *Gargoyle*: "The River"; *Laurel Review*: "The Ways Things Are"; *Margie*: "I Like to Stay Home," "Understanding Fiction"; *Poems & Plays*: "CHiPs," "The Fighting Poets," "Chinatown Book of the Dead"; *Rattle*: "Getting Tough With John Ruskin"; *Rivendale*: "Do You Have Any Advice for Those of Us Starting Out?"; *River Styx*: "All Hallows Eve," "Collinsville," "Cosmos 2219"; *Smartish Pace*: "Summer '62," "The Abominable Snowman"; *Solo*: "Elsewhere," "Lot's Wife," "A Day in the Life"

Contents

I

II

More people than I can name have been important to me over the years. Publishers and editors, of course. Naturally my wife and my friends. But also those who sat down to write me a nice note or who said something charming after a reading. You know who you are, and this book is for you, too.

I

Kryptonite

Lois liked to see the bullets bounce
off Superman's chest, and of course
she was proud when he leaned into
a locomotive and saved the crippled
orphan who had fallen on the tracks.

Yet on those long nights when he was
readjusting longitude or destroying
a meteor headed right for some nun,
Lois considered carrying just a smidgen
of kryptonite in her purse or at least
making a tincture to dab behind her ears.

She pictured his knees giving way,
the color draining from his cheeks.
He'd lie on the couch like a guy with
the flu, too weak to paint the front
porch or take out the garbage. She
could peek down his tights or draw
on his chest with a ball point. She
might even muss his hair and slap
him around.

"Hey, what'd I do?" he'd croak
just like a regular boyfriend. At last.

Early

At the post office, all I can do is stare
through locked glass as sleepy clerks
puzzle over a crude address, then file
it among the other mysteries.

Trader Joe's isn't open yet, either.
I wait among banked flowers while
a clerk discards drowsy forsythia,
pours tart water at my feet.

I might actually be early to my own
funeral — peeking into the guest
register, stealing behind the scenes
where a busy mortician has left half
a cup of Sanka, admiring the new suit
already installed in that beguiling luge.

In spring, I'll bet the grass above me
will be green first, stunning even
the young gardener who eyes
my wife, her breath silver-white
above the vivid blades.

Understanding Fiction

I poured Goldy into the carrier, the one
with the cartoon cat on the side.

Dr. Pio took one look and said, "Oh,
she's so sick." Then he used that amorous
phrase, "We'll put her to sleep."

When I got home, everybody was reading.
The covers of the books were lurid:
a dagger dripped blood, people clung
to one another.

My little story wouldn't stand a chance.

Collinsville

My Uncle Max lived by himself in a little place
        on Blythe Street, not far from the bell
factory. He was my mother's brother, the baby
        of the family. I was an only child,
oldest and youngest at the same time.
        My mother wanted us both to settle down.
For me that meant practicing piano or reading
        Longfellow, anything but bouncing a ball
off the side of the house. For Uncle Max it meant
        some nice girl my mother had dug up.
"But Ada," he'd say, "I don't want a *nice* girl."
        She'd be just as shocked every time
and my father would smile a little and tuck himself
        into the evening *Star*.

Uncle Max could do anything with cars. He liked
        his work and went at it seven days a week
until one winter he got sick. My mother nursed him
        and while she had him down talked about who
would do this next time because she wouldn't be
        around forever and there he'd be in that
drafty shack and she knew this girl . . .

        Mom must have scared him good, because
when he was up and around, he married Iris Wood
        who had worked down at the Black & White
Cleaners for as long as I could remember.

Iris took to marriage. She got a phone and ordered
        food to go. Max just dove into the alligator
mouths of Packards and stayed there until one
        day he went to St. Louis for a rebuilt
fuel pump and came back with a woman. They were
        out at the Moonlight Motel for almost two
weeks. Then I heard that the woman had run off.
        I wasn't sure what they meant so I pictured her
pounding down the frontage road with everything bouncing.

Mother said I was too young, but Dad took me with
        him to get Uncle Max. I'd never seen the inside
of a motel room before. There was a bed with sheets
        piled in the middle like the last of a snowman.
There were bottles all over, half a box of chocolates,
        and White Castle wrappers. Uncle Max cried
when we dropped him off in front of his house and
        Dad gave him some money.

That night Mother said it was a shame what had
        happened to Max, how he'd married that good
for nothing Iris and then made a bigger fool of himself.
        My father put the paper down. He said she
should drop the subject. Wasn't she satisfied? Hadn't
        she done enough? By God, he never wanted to
hear another word about it ever again.

He froze the room. He'd never shouted in his life
        except for one other time when I came
back from playing baseball. I had won the game
        and I said what a nice little town this was
and that maybe I would just stay here forever.

Myths

Today my mother says she is afraid of turning into
a vegetable. I know what she means, but the way
she says it reminds me of Greek myths where
people became poplar trees and cows.

I imagine being called to the hospital and there,
under a light blanket, is a huge zucchini. I struggle
to make sense of it even if that means embracing
the randomness of willful gods.

But the doctor can't keep a straight face. He bites
the inside of his lip to keep from laughing. I can
hardly blame him. It's not his mother lying there
with a stem.

Well, probably she won't turn into anything
distressing. Not that Mom hasn't had her share
of greed or ambition or longing, but she's very
healthy. In fact, she's been in the hospital
only once—the night I was born.

Halfway through the delivery, she thought she saw
God's face on the ceiling. Then it turned into a Chrysler.
"I didn't know which to believe in," she confides.
"I still don't."

CHiPS

Usually Ponch is pure high spirits, the cop
who needs a sidekick like John to keep him
out of trouble.

But in today's episode, he's afraid to ride
his motorcycle fast. He sends John after
that speeding Camaro then ducks into an alley.
He looks right into the camera and uses his
other expression to show how upset he is.
The only thing that gets Ponch out of this
funk is the news on his crackling radio:
John is in trouble! He puts on his sunglasses
in that cool two-handed way, then hauls ass
out of there.

At dinner that night with two grade school
teachers, Ponch's date plays with his hair
and feeds him shrimp. John tells the brunette
that before he started working out in high
school, he was the kind of kid who almost
never got off the school bus without somebody
writing HOMO on his lunchbox. When he was
paired up with Ponch, he thought it'd never
work, but it did. They're good together.

John's date smiles. She knows boys like
this from her school, boys who are inseparable,
who always have their arms around each
other and even when they have to go home
for dinner call right after to see what's
going on.

Reentry Women

They were very nervous the first days, clutching their new texts. Some had already made covers out of paper bags, but these weren't decorated with hearts or phone numbers. They just kept the books clean.

They were easy to teach: cooperative, diligent, polite. Even at the break most stayed in the room, doing homework or chatting. One of these went to a palm reader, and took some of her classmates. I heard them quoting Madame Slovic, what she said about a man who was coming back soon and how different he would be.

They were all, it seemed, separated or divorced, and most had mean, jealous husbands. Some of these came on campus, and one burst into the room. I threatened him with—it was all I had—an eraser before the women rose as one and he ran.

I didn't mind that they lied for each other about disconnected phones and babysitters who did not show up. Eventually someone would come up to the desk and admit that Sheila or Kinisha or Trudy had disappeared.

For the final, they brought things to eat. I handed back the last essays. We all shook hands. Many had done well, most had passed, but it was still a melancholy afternoon made more so by the movie I happened onto when I got home.

It was a sci-fi film where rocket ships plummeted through space. Reentering the Earth's atmosphere, they shook violently. The astronauts inside hung on for dear life, their features contorted. And a few ships—pursued or pursuer, it was hard to tell—couldn't bear up under the strain and flew apart.

St. Stephen's Day

During Christmas, my parents invited the barber
to dinner because he did not have a family.
In Collinsville, living alone was worse than
cancer. That someone could be solitary
by nature was as heretical as the idea
that God had big feet and took baths.

Today I have a pork chop marinating
and a bottle of good wine. I should eat
on the patio. It's beautiful out and so quiet
it's almost like the world is waiting for God
to finish bathing, to put on the secret music,
and to finally dance with the enormous jury
of His peers.

Shame

I have been practicing the first two
lines of a poem by Chung Ling:

"I make fast my white barge
To the bank of the brimming stream."

One of my students wrote it out for me
phonetically. I want to say these lines

to the old Chinese guys I swim
with every afternoon at the Y.

I think they would enjoy it. I think
they would like me. Today there is

no one in the pool but us, and we
are all hanging onto the sides.

I point to the placid water and recite.
They are stunned, and then Mr. Chu

starts to weep. His friends help him
out. They disappear through the blue

door. Later there is a note on my locker,
written on a paper towel, written with

such passion the paper is torn, written
in a language they think I understand.

The Abominable Snowman

Up here on the forehead of the world, it's always
cold. On the other hand, there's very little crime.

My wife and I live in a cave way above the snow
line. It's a simple life with no distractions to

speak of. There's lots of foraging. Otherwise
we practice nonchalance. For fun, we leave

footprints and sometimes intriguing scat
a cameraman has to take a close-up of.

There's always a cameraman, part of a team:
someone in a Nessie baseball hat, and this time

ardent Nora who wants to be the first woman
to photograph us. She thinks the men have

gone about it all wrong and her notes, pinned
to a glacier, are charming: *Help me believe !*

And *I have fire. Really.* In her journal, which I
pilfer while they sleep or hike, Nora's worried

about her hair. She's planned an assignation
with a man she met on the plane. Well, well.

Someone handsomer than I, no doubt. Still,
I like her, so I grunt into a tape recorder

before I leave and urinate in a hat, not the one
she planned to wear for her rendezvous in Bhutan,

I hope.

Getting Tough with John Ruskin

The lady at the reference desk just called
to say that *Seven Lamps of Architecture*
finally came in, so even though it's raining
I have to put on my turquoise polo because
picking up a new book is a little like
meeting someone for the first time, though
I certainly don't want Ruskin lighting my
cigarette and asking where I found a shirt
that so perfectly matched my eyes, the way
Oscar Wilde did last week.

I wouldn't even read Ruskin if I didn't have
to. He was the jerk who thought all naked
women were going to look like the marble
statues in museums. So when Effie Gray
turned out to have pubic hair he was horrified
and the marriage was never consummated.

Well, I'll tell you what, Johnny. I'll drive
over to the library and pick up your book,
but if I don't like what I see *muy rapido*
it's back where you came from. And if
you thought industrial England in 1862
was ugly, wait'll you see the bottom
of a book drop on a day like this!

Saturday Morning

When the dog won't stop barking, I meet
my neighbors in front of the blue house.

It's early and in our pajamas and robes
we look like delegates from the Land of Nod.

Someone pounds on the door as the sky
darkens with the black Lab's consonants.

Then we shrug and go home to lie rigid
as fossils, or maybe make love to

the steady hectoring like couples at some
Fascist bordello, or perhaps just turn

on the TV and find Pluto banned to the back
yard. Mickey frowns over the yellow fence.

The last time he heard a racket like that
Minnie was having a nervous breakdown.

He certainly hopes history isn't about
to repeat itself.

Reading the School Literary Magazine

Rose Ann's sonnet finally has socks
that match. Ben's "Ode to Summer"
poses in seersucker pants and spotless
bucks while Richard's aubade sports
a crest on the pajama pocket.

But I miss those pedal pushers
with the cheerful rip, that lucky
Padres' cap, the T-shirt from Bangkok.

And what happened to Louise—her dreamy,
id-driven odyssey? Look at it now: pearls,
a modest collar, those big daunting buttons.

After Sun Yum Feng

Homesick for the wealth I once possessed,
I drive through the best part of town.
Beautiful children in white stand politely
until a shadow opens their car door.
A wisp of smoke rises from one chimney,
perhaps someone burning a love letter.
I am such a fool, but I pull to the curb
and write this down, anyway.

Found

My wife waits for a caterpillar
to crawl onto her palm so she
can carry it out of the street
and into the green subdivision
of a tree.

Yesterday she coaxed a spider
into a juicier corner. The day
before she hazed a snail
in a half-circle so he wouldn't
have to crawl all the way
around the world and be 2000
years late for dinner.

I want her to hurry up and pay
attention to me or go where I
want to go until I remember
the night she found me wet
and limping, felt for a collar
and tags, then put me in
the truck where it was warm.

Without her, I wouldn't
be standing here in these
snazzy, alligator shoes.

The Consolations of Cinema

Some people drown in vodka or jazz. I like
an enormous eyeball first.

This one travels in a cloud, no doubt to make
a better first impression, like a fat man
in vertical stripes. At first there's just
a lot of hikers saying, "Gosh, what's that?"
Then blood-curdling screams.

Eventually we see the monster, predictably
huge and icky but it is, after all, just an eye.
You'd think a handful of sand or a really bright
light would do the trick. Much less running
at it with scissors.

But I've forgotten the radioactivity, a staple
in 50's horror films. So Mr. Handsome has to call
in the air force and the menace writhes and dies.

They always writhe and die. Or melt or slink back
into the depths, mortally wounded. There's never
a funeral for monsters. The dreadful never stand
in the rain singing, "Come, ye Disconsolate."

I need to get out of these dark clothes.
I need to get out period. Somewhere
there's a waitress with beautiful knees,
Stoly straight up, Anita O'Day
on the best jukebox in town.

Adult Video Arcade

In this one, the patron goes downstairs
to his own little booth, which is clean
and dry. There's a guy in a blue T-shirt
that reads SECURITY. Sometimes he's
amiable, but today he's barking at
an old man fumbling in the semi-dark.
I take his arm like a Boy Scout. After
a dead end or two, I get him to booth #23,
where he sits down gratefully and a little
short of breath. This, by the way, is my birthday.

My movie is shot mostly outdoors. At one
point a dog trots by and I wonder whom he
belongs to. Then a bird flies into the shot,
sits on the nearest branch, and begins
to sing. The sound man, probably bored to death,
swings the boom that way. The song is plaintive
and, it seems to me, full of yearning.

On my way out, I feel like I should stop
at booth #23 and make sure everything
is okay, the way my parents would drop by
the house of a widower from church
and take a casserole or a pie. SECURITY
wouldn't understand. Anyway, the place
is busier, full of shadowy figures,
one of whom lights matches to find his
way and draws a sharp rebuke from the guard.

My wife has organized a party, so tonight
I'll see my friends. I show myself that movie:
"Turning 65." I think of other turns
I have taken. There's no way to retrace
my steps, the hedge closes what's behind me.
That sounds scary but someone's singing
on the other side of the tall, sculpted
box elder. I'm alone but people are forever
passing me with a nod or walking alongside
for awhile or deciding to lie down on one
of the marble benches, everybody making
their way toward the center which may be
really awful but there are those who
believe it's completely sunny there
with a view of just about everything.

II

Since You Asked

I'd say my style is conversational, or maybe loquacious
like someone trying to pledge a good sorority, someone
who can't stop talking about her stuffed animals.

Still, I'll bet there's plenty of what people call hidden
meaning in my work. Not that I'd know. I've heard
Frost's "Stopping By Woods on a Snowy Evening"
is about Death, but why couldn't it be about Weather
or Real Estate?

I'm terrible at ferreting out meanings, though I admire
people who can lean into a sonnet with their stethoscopes
and then deliver the news with the same grave expression
as physicians.

For the kind of poems I'm writing now, I'm glad I wasn't
born in Japan. I can see my haiku master fanning himself
as I count the syllables and say, "Two hundred and ten."

No, I'm an American, and a long-winded one. I just go on
like one of those blue highways through Montana with
an occasional joke or simile like a roadside attraction.

Other poets tug on the reins and pause in the dark. Inside
their mittens they count perfect iambs. They think deep
thoughts while snow fills the ruts the sleigh left
and collects on the brims of their somber hats.

Teen Jesus

There are a few apocryphal stories about Jesus as a child:
how He walked up a sunbeam and flabbergasted His
playmates, how His bath water could cure any illness.

But there are no stories about Him as a teenager.
Did He make His bed without being told, or was He
the kind of boy who jumped out from behind bushes,
scaring girls on their way to the well, making
them drop those picturesque amphoras.

Did Mary nag Him about outgrowing His robes
and sandals: "Jesus, do You think Your father
and I are made out of myrrh?"

He was probably a cool kid, one the others looked up to.
It wasn't only that He said He wouldn't live very long.
A lot of the guys said that, especially the ones who
drank too much wine and raced their donkeys. Jesus
was different. While everybody else partied by the Dead
Sea, he'd take the rowboat out, step right off the bow,
and sink like a stone. Then he'd swim back in all mad.

His pals could tease Him out of a bad mood, though.
Pretty soon, He'd change water into beer and make one
hot dog feed everybody. Girls liked him, but He wasn't
into them, though no way was He like Obadiah, who made
his own curtains.

Nobody was surprised when He left home. A few
almost tagged along. But they couldn't resist Esther's
long hair pulled back and fastened with an amber pin,
or the pale underside of Miriam's wrist. They married
and never went more than five miles from Nazareth.

Cinderella's Diary

I miss my stepmother. What a thing to say
but it's true. The prince is so boring: four
hours to dress and then the cheering throngs.
Again. The page who holds the door is cute
enough to eat. Where is he once Mr. Charming
kisses my forehead goodnight?

Every morning I gaze out a casement window
at the hunters, dark men with blood on their
boots who joke and mount, their black trousers
straining, rough beards, callused hands, selfish,
abrupt . . .

Oh, dear diary—I am lost in ever after:
those insufferable birds, someone in every
room with a lute, the queen calling me to look
at another painting of her son, this time
holding the transparent slipper I wish
I'd never seen.

Losing My Religion

At the Illinois State Fair, I was given five dollars
and allowed to roam the midway. I didn't want cotton
candy or a corn dog. I wasn't old enough for French Follies.

Then I saw a kid carrying a giant panda that
looked like a god other prizes might pray to.
Of course, I lost all my money and didn't win
a thing. Moping around, though, I saw
the same kid slip between tents, return
the panda to a grizzled carny, and get paid.

I was a sensitive child, the sort of little pantywaist
who might grow up to be a poet, so I burst into tears.
A policeman led me to the Pavilion of Lost Children.
I cried loudest of all and refused the awful cookie.

By the time my parents found me, I was running a fever,
and my father drove home disgusted, getting a speeding
ticket which he blames me for to this very day.

Flying to Nevada with
Ten Thousand Dollars in My Sock

The man across the aisle from me looks like Henry
James. He even writes without lifting his pen,
glancing up every now with a frown, perhaps
wishing he had gone a little easier on the assonance
of "to be led to the marriage bed was to be dead."

My students don't like Henry James; the damage
is too meticulous. And maybe they're right. Maybe
an explosion or two and a car chase would perk
up *The Golden Bowl*.

I didn't like HJ either when I was young. But after
a few divorces and some rehab I am happy to follow
his sentences like the paths of an English garden
that lead to a bench with gargoyle arms.

The plane banks, and there are the lights of The Strip.
Henry James called Italy "the vomitorium of America."
I'm sure Las Vegas has surpassed that by now.

Faux Henry adjusts his seatbelt. He glances over
and licks his lips and I'm reminded of James' letter
to John Addington Symonds: "It seemed to me that
the victims of a common passion should sometimes
exchange a look."

I Like to Stay Home

I like to walk out front and look at the Mexican
sage or to the west side of the house where
my neighbor Jim has put in some new leaded
glass decorated with roses.

Around back is a clothesline, usually hung with
laundry. It's very pleasant to sit on the steps
with one of the cats and watch the breeze move
a blouse hung upside down like an acrobat.

My friends go to Bangkok and the Black Forest,
but I settle for house and yard, a dozen
amaryllis, garbage cans with numbers on them,
a possum to summon me back to this world.

At two a.m. I get up and go outside in my white
pajamas. Above is the butter-colored moon,
underfoot crushed mint. Over there is the possum
so I tell him to shoo, go home.

I clap my hands like a lady at court applauding
the harpsichord, and follow his tail around
the corner. Jim has left a light on, and there
are those roses, the ones that never get to
drop their petals on a blue tablecloth
like they do at my house.

Summer, 1962

When I worked at the library, my favorite job
was opening up in the morning. Strolling toward
the big, wooden doors I felt like the manager
in a store of ideas.

If it weren't for those long hours at the desk, I might
still be there. But I not only watched the days pass,
I marked each one with an indelible stamp.

When I told the head librarian, he was disappointed.
"Should you change your mind," he said, "your job
will be waiting."

He sounded like the vicar in a book about a plucky
but misguided lad who goes off to the city.
I pictured my job waiting for me at the crossroads
or lying by the grave of the person I almost was,
its face on its paws.

Queer Benediction

Herbert lived across the street with his mother and his
aunt. He took a lot of baths then sat on the steps with his
hair in a towel, swami-style. He smoked a lot, too, and held
a Chesterfield between thumb and forefinger, palm up. "As
they do," he said, "on the continent." He was twenty-eight
years old and didn't have a job.

My mother told me to never use the bathroom at Herbert's
or go into the garage with him alone. I could sit on the porch
with Aunt Mabel, but when she went inside for more lemonade
Herbert always talked about the poet Shelley—the genius.
Or he might ask me to sit half in sun half in shade and turn
just so.

In our town, the men worked and drank. Coming home
from the tavern once my father charged the porch, tore me
from the striped canvas chair, and held me up like a lantern.
That was the night Mrs. Alexander threw her husband's things
on the lawn. All the neighbors gathered to look at the long
johns, work shoes, half a carton of Kools, and the dead
rooster her husband had raised from a chick.

Herbert put his palm on my head. "Oh, honey," he said, "promise
me you'll get out of this town."

Stanza in Italian Means Room

Even the foyer is attractive, with its
blue tile and enchanted mirror.

Who wouldn't like that leather couch,
long as an alexandrine.

Or the dining room with its canary
and heavily padlocked armoire.

The kitchen is perfect, especially
the mangled sweater by the toaster.

I even like the laundry room: those
Maytags, that almost mounted trout.

American Wife

I have been reading Chinese poems.
I like the ones where a woman makes
love to her husband while thinking
of a place beyond the mountains
where even the snow is intact.

That's what I do. That's what I did
just before the barbecue. When
the boys drift indoors to caress
the steaks, my sister-in-law
does a line or two and cries.

I think of the poem where a girl
named Ch'ang-O flees to the moon
for refuge.

Now covered by men's footprints,
we wouldn't be safe even there.

Cosmos 2219

I drive up Angeles Crest Highway, ease the little truck
        into #26 at Silver Moccasin Campground
and stretch my legs. Lots of tents and fires. A family
        argues in Thai as they arrange blue Igloo
coolers and canvas chairs. A couple of girls kissing
        at a bare table scowl at me, and the skinny one
holds a flashlight under her chin so she looks horrible like
        some kid at camp trying to scare the crybabies.

My wife's sleeping bag still smells like her, so I slip in
        and lie down in the back of the truck. A satellite
goes over and I glance at the What's Happening in Heaven
        Tonight schedule. There's Cosmos 2219, right on time.
Some people believe those satellites are monitoring our
        every move, just as God was once supposed to monitor
our every thought. When He got to me I imagined Him
        frowning at Betti Page in her skimpy cat suit.

When people died back then, our pastor said the good ones
        went to Heaven where everything was taken
care of, nobody had arthritis, nobody had to get up at 6:00
        to start a fire. Which sounded a lot like Hawaii
because those who could afford it always said, "Oh, it's so
        beautiful and warm and we never had to lift a finger."

I try to imagine some of the dead people I know in that heaven.
        Jack would get along fine. He liked sitting around
while good-looking boys brought him things. I'm not so sure
        about Dad. Waiters intimidated him, but I think any
heaven worth its salt would have a cafeteria. And I can easily
        see my grandma, who died changing a light bulb,
sweeping the streets of gold in front of her mansion.

All around me, people settle down. I hear the long zippers
of sleeping bags. A baby cries. A girl laughs
and says, "Stop that!" The mountain, full of amputated trees,
sighs. Another satellite goes by winking like
a weary roué. But no falling stars. So I give up and head home.
I'm on the freeway when there's this meteor
shower with a huge radiant drift. Wouldn't you know it: an
hour each way and the big show goes on one minute
from home.

As I turn into the driveway, I imagine Jack and Dad standing on
clouds like folks in a cartoon, but instead of Zeus-
bolts, they're tossing meteors. Jack will always be young
and limber, so it's easy for him to pinpoint the Castro
and then Green Valley where his parents live. Dad's arthritis
is gone, and he has a wicked sidearm that carries
right over Collinsville where Mom can see it. Grandma is
up on another ladder, a brand new star in her hand.

But this time she doesn't fall. Only the star slips and lights
up the sky over the garage. My friends at Moccasin
Flats must see it, too: the ranger brooding in his green truck,
the skinny girl who likes kissing, the Thai father
smoking one last bitter cigarette.

Weather

Some of my friends claim they could
never live in California. They find
the regular beauty too much like
a postcard with its predictable
tanka.

And, anyway, how do I ever get
anything done with the sun luring
everyone to the first tee
or the pari-mutuel windows,

much less the way the chairs
all seem to lean back under a tree,
a cat ready to curl up on my lap
or at my sandaled feet.

They prefer the bracing rigors
of snow and rain. They write
about its feet and inches, all
they endure to buy an orange
or see a movie as they

picture me, probably, still on
my chaise, their letter falling
from one languid hand onto
the voluptuous lawn.

Body Shop

When I come in, my mechanic is eating
lunch. He doesn't look over the top
of his newspaper.

I glance around, hoping that Miss July
with her sassy fife will distract me,
but his calendars

feature only a vernal wrench, perky
timing belt, naked carburetor:
things that might make a robot humid.

Sitting across from his headlines, I feel
like the mechanic's wife: virtues ignored,
faults magnified, taken for granted . . .

It's all I can do to not clutch
the lapels of my robe and run into
the bathroom weeping.

Finally he listens. Intently. Leaning closer,
one hand on my trembling manifold.

Annunciation at Pico and Sixth

My partner and I pull over this possible
DUI and run her plates. It's just routine,
but something about the way she looks
in all that hopped-up light reminds me
of what my art teacher said that time
I went to city college:

In bad paintings nothing fazes Mary.
Not the wattage, not the angel, *nada.*
But in good ones, she's like this
blonde—half-blind, a little scared,
pretty sure she hasn't done anything
to deserve all this.

The River

It's a little early for Mrs. Dalloway's party,
so I chat with my students. They went
here and there over the weekend, saw this
and that. Me? I worked in the garden, turning
over an astonishing number of worms.

"Gee," says Laura. "Since you're a poet,
that must have made you think of death
and stuff."

Death & Stuff: it sounds like some
awful boutique selling Yorick's skull
in designer colors, Sylvia's oven mittens,
and replicas of the *S.S. Orizaba* including
a toy Hart Crane to bob in its wake.

Suddenly I feel like the kind of poet
Laura means, the kind who throws himself
on a chaise and says, "I grow weary."

Instead, I reach into the river that runs through
my classroom, fill both pockets with rocks,
and step into the first class of the day.

The Boogeyman

Women stayed home under the garlic,
children cowered in a corner with the goat.
Men whittled stakes, poured silver
bullets and assembled a mob.

When they returned, there was wine
and sighs of relief. Windows flung open
to receive a virginal breeze. Everybody
went back to work.

But pretty soon boys start hanging out
by the fountain again, smoking weeds
and making fun of their parents' hats.
Girls stain their lips with berries
and wash each other's feet.

That's when Ivan drags in a sheep
with its throat ripped open. Katrina sees
lights in the old castle, and the coachman
says he delivered three coffins.

The kids look at each other. Even if they left
at dawn, night would overtake them. And they
can't leave at dawn. They've got chores to do.

Mr. & Mrs. Horse

were eating dinner. Mr. Horse had his
nostrils deep in the Farm Report.
"At least it's a good day for the race."

Mrs. Horse looked up, a forkful of hay
halfway to her lips which resemble
yours with hormone trouble. "What
race is that?"

"The human race." Mr. Horse chortled
and slobbered. "That's a good one."

Mrs. Horse sighed. Who could blame her
for yesterday in Room 309 of the Holiday
Inn, nervously sipping champagne
and thinking thoughts of love which
resemble yours with no trouble at all.

Nancy Drew

Merely pretty, she made up for it with vim.
And she got to say things like, "But, gosh,
what if these plans should fall into the wrong
hands?" And it was pretty clear she didn't mean
plans for a party or a trip to the museum, but
something involving espionage and a Nazi or two.

In fact, the handsome exchange student turns
out to be a Fascist sympathizer. When he snatches
Nancy along with some blueprints, she knows he
has something more sinister in mind than kissing
with his mouth open.

Locked in the pantry of an abandoned farm house,
Nancy makes a radio out of a shoelace and a muffin.
Pretty soon the police show up, and everything's
hunky dory.

Nancy accepts their thanks, but she's subdued.
It's not like her to fall for a cad. Even as she plans
a short vacation to sort out her emotions she knows
there will be a suspicious waiter, a woman in a green
off the shoulder dress, and her very jittery husband.

Very well. But no more handsome boys like the last one:
the part in his hair that was sheer propulsion, that way
he had of lifting his eyes to hers over the custard,
those feelings that made her not want to be brave
confident and daring, polite, sensitive and caring.

Blue

The director changes the sheets
himself, tucks in a fitted bottom,
turns back the top one, and sighs.

"This is a threesome," he says, "so
it's you over here, Suzanne. You down
there, Bob. And Meg, wherever, okay?"

It's pretty early, but we try hard.
Once it was cops and jail time. Now it's
AIDS and all that stuff.

But if you're careful it pays the bills
and then some. It's almost never as
sick as the stuff you see on TV,

and every now and then it's really
lovely, one of those kindnesses
nobody understands.

III

MAN vs. NATURE

The Olympic is packed. Spotlights cross
like swords in the smoky air. Every few
minutes, a new blonde glides toward
the front row and the crowd moans
with envy and desire.

Then Nature starts down the aisle sneering
as he adjusts his leafy trunks and cape
of Spanish moss. The crowd eats him up:
cheering, leaning for a high-five, waving
banners with red, dripping letters.

Almost no one notices Man, puny even
in a fur parka. He parts the ropes himself,
then plops onto a stool.

The money is pouring in on Nature because
he is huge and beautiful and awesome.
But a few in the crowd know that Man
is wily and resilient. He can sharpen
a stick and make fire.

So the wise guys take three to one
and sit back, only glancing away from
the action when the blondes yawn
and stand to adjust the dead mink
draped around their voracious shoulders.

The Way Things Are

The night nurse has my cell phone number.
So I go to *La Boheme* because my niece
is in it and I promised.

It's hot in Paris. The bohemians sweat,
and their make-up runs. Mimi coughs
into a red handkerchief.

A few dads take pictures, single moms
fan themselves with programs and eye
the tall boy in the chorus, the one
with the dagger in his boot.

The way things are, I'm not surprised that
I can see inside everyone on stage. I can see
the flames in their hearts. Some are red
and vigorous, others small but steady, one
or two barely there, blue and vulnerable
as pilot lights.

The boy playing Rodolpho steps forward
carrying a candle and starts to sing.
For the first time tonight, the room quiets.

The janitor looks up from his racing paper.
Even the thugs in the back here for extra
credit stop thinking of their innocent dicks
for a minute and listen.

Lot's Wife

She'd been told not to look back. But her husband
was always telling somebody not to do something,
always lecturing the children, or storming over
to make the neighbors turn down their music.

So of course they played louder and thought up
new jokes about his weight (quite a Lot),
his dreamy, pious expression (vacant Lot),
or the putative size of his member (not a Lot).

They weren't bad people, just high-spirited.
She'd grown up with many of them, slept over
at her girlfriend's, dated boys who whispered
her name. How did she end up as nothing
but Lot's wife?

And then those angels stopped at her house
and when the Sodomities came for them, Lot
offered his daughters instead.

Who in his right mind would do that?
And who could live with him then.

Whom Do You See as Your Ideal Reader?

Maybe someone pouring a first cup of coffee,
smoothing an alarming ATM voucher and puzzling
over an incriminating Polaroid with a phone number
on the back.

Or perhaps it's the beautiful and petulant, tired
of modeling one teddy after another and refusing
to eat even butter lettuce until she has finished
my collected works.

Of course, there is always the Platonic reader:
comfortable chair, good light, my latest
on a Mission Oak table beside a steaming cup
of Earl Gray.

Then I remember that Plato didn't trust poets,
so now my ideal reader has to leave the Republic
and cross the border to a lesser country, one
lit mostly by neon. He must be brave enough

to step into a store full of sheepish men
and ask in a whisper for my poems, his heart
pounding as the tattooed clerk looks both ways
then reaches under the counter where he keeps
the good stuff.

Calendar

It's the first of the year, time to transfer things
from my old calendar into the new one. I feel a little
like Janus, pointing my beard first into the past then
the future.

There's a nephew's birthday in February which is,
by the way, from *februum* (purification), though he
is so young his indiscretions involve little more
than a dismembered Barbi or playing with matches.

April is the cruelest months for my cats. They hate
their Advantage flea treatment. And I have to open wide
(*aperio*) for my dental hygienist.

May (Maia, goddess of bounty) is one of my favorite months,
because the Kentucky Derby is in early May, and someone
who bets like I do needs all the bounty he can get.

June is Juno's month, and my niece who told her mother
she wanted a red wedding dress with a turquoise bodice
and train might like to know that one of Juno's symbols
is the peacock. Another is the cow, and the less said
about that the better.

But now the task turns melancholy, as it must have
for those naming the months because they quickly
settled for a couple of Caesars (Julius and Augustus)
and numbers seven through ten of the old Roman calendar.

I think we all know what it's like to hurry through
unhappy times. With me it was July: phone call,
plane trip, cemetery, a taxi idling at the entrance,
its inevitable meter running.

Career Move

I've handled a lot of fighters in my day, good
ones too. Legit contenders. Until some pretty
boy from Calexico buys the farm and there
that goes. So just for walking around money,
I take on some verbs for the Your Word
Against Mine smoker at MLA.

At first it's all right: Verbs are easy to
handle. They're used to pointing, so the jab
is second nature. And I get a good match:
some guy's Old French with one of mine
who goes all the way back to ME.

Friday night, I shake hands with the money,
get a good seat, tell the guy in front of me
to take off his goddamned mortarboard or
else. On the undercard, an article takes out
a preposition in two. Some adjective from
Fresno decisions the local adverb. But
I gotta tell you, without the cleavage
on that deconstructionist in the first
row, I'm asleep.

Just then a guy who used to spar for me
sits down, says there's somebody he'd
like me to meet. Next thing I know, I'm
shaking hands with this tricked out gerund.
Okay, I'm new to this part of the business,
but even I know you never touch a fucking
gerund. They're nothing but trouble.

So I just walk away. Literally. Next morning
I go downtown, get a thirty day emergency
teaching credential. I start tomorrow at
the community college right up the street.

The Nine Muses

Certainly Thalia could keep them in stitches, all except for
Milpomene who always had the corners of her pretty mouth
turned down. As Tragedy's muse, did she handle only *King Lear*
and the Joad family, or did she find time for a girl sitting
in front of her mirror on prom night, unable to do anything
with her hair?

Clio had all of History to take care of, but I like to think she
also whispered the dates of the Pelopennisian War to a stumped
fourth-grader just as Polyhymnia, goddess of Rhetoric and
Geometry, guided the hand of the boy drawing his first
isosceles triangle.

Is Terpsichore the most popular of the muses? All the little girls
at Toe Tap & Jazz worship her, and there is always the club scene
on Saturday night.

Calliope is always looking for someone who has the big shoulders
for epic poetry, though most of the bound journals with hand-pressed
pages she peeks into begin, "I sit alone." But she likes the thin,
jittery boy in the corner of the coffee house, so she calls Erato and
Euterpe to help him describe the forearm of the waitress who delivers
his many lattes.

All that is left is Urania. She knew Ptolemy and Copernicus and
is responsible for today's Antennae Galaxies and Deep Hubble Field.
But she doesn't forget the graduate student on his own near midnight
who feels sweet breath in his ear, a light touch on his wrinkled sleeve.
With rising excitement he strides to the eyepiece and sees everything
he has seen before, but suddenly in a new configuration
and charged with meaning.

Fever

Delores Del Rio takes a walking tour
of my body. Unlike most vagabonds
in sturdy boots and a stained rucksack,
Delores wears a red dress and slingbacks.

She hums the arsonist's theme
as she taps one coy organ after another
and makes them tawdry with flame.

When she gets a little tired,
she sits on my spleen and smokes.
If she glanced up, she'd see
two aspirin careening toward her

like the lights of a very small car
destined to disappear in a fiery crash.

The Styx

Some stand on the bank and fish. Others want
to be baptized and step gingerly into dark
water while the choir in their mangled bus
begins "Shall We Gather at the River."

A couple of kids—he's been working out
but is still self-conscious in Speedos,
she's stunning in a hemorrhage-red
bikini—dive off a crag holding hands.

A honey bun, a precious little sweetie pie
plays in the shallows while Mom reads
People and dozes.

Some say they heard the shot, others no.
A few were driving, most never saw it coming.
That man waited too long to see the doctor.
This one went in the wrong door. The bus driver
with his name on the pocket went to sleep.

The ferry crosses every hour. Its wake rocks
the fat man in his inner tube who thinks he
hears the rapids again, but no —it's just
the rumble of motorcycles last seen racing
on Angeles Crest.

The boy bleeding from the face and neck tries
to pet Cerebrus who growls then remembers going
to the world of the living with Hercules:
the acres of green, the sticks anyone might
throw, the miracle of a red ball.

"Do You Have Any Advice
For Those of Us Just Starting Out?"

Give up sitting dutifully at your desk. Leave
your house or apartment. Go out into the world.

It's all right to carry a notebook but a cheap
one is best, with pages the color of weak tea
and on the front a kitten or a space ship.

Avoid any enclosed space where more than
three people are wearing turtlenecks. Beware
any snow-covered chalet with deer tracks
across the muffled tennis courts.

Not surprisingly, libraries are a good place to write.
And the perfect place in a library is near an aisle
where a child a year or two old is playing as his
mother browses the ranks of the dead.

Often he will pull books from the bottom shelf.
The title, the author's name, the brooding photo
on the flap mean nothing. Red book on black, gray
book on brown, he builds a tower. And the higher
it gets, the wider he grins.

You who asked for advice, listen: When the tower
falls, be like that child. Laugh so loud everybody
in the world frowns and says, "Shhhh."

Then start again.

The Chinatown Book of the Dead

Beside me is a box that says Candied Squid.
Across the room a small shrine with oranges
and incense. Eyes half-closed in concentration,
a new Chinese doctor is taking my pulses.
"Kidneys weak," he says. "Not serious."

My old Chinese doctor used to ask about my sex
life. "How power?" he'd say, raising his forearm
and clenched fist. So I brought him a poem by
a 9th century concubine which began, "All you
can do is mumble."

Dr. Xi laughed uproariously and told everyone
in Tin Bo Herbs & Pharmaceuticals. Even the old
ladies leaning on their dutiful sons smiled.

When I went back in September, he didn't stand
up to greet me. He listened, wrote out another
prescription, then put both hands on my forehead
and said good-bye.

I don't think he will have a hard time in the bardos,
looking with mere affection at the beautiful young
girls, with tolerance at the piles of silk and gold.

Only one thing might tempt him to slip into yet
another body, and that is the rheumy eyes and
heavy breathing of the ill, our hands extended,
wrists exposed, and beneath the skin
the insistent pulse.

Steve McQueen

Though he was known for those ice-blue eyes and general
            sang-froid, he is remembered in some circles
mostly for *The Blob*, his first movie. This was quite
            a bit after he'd replaced Ben Gazzara in *A Hatful
of Rain* but right on the heels of *Wanted – Dead or Alive*
            where he played the laconic Josh Randall and wore
that peculiar sidearm, a sort of sawed-off rifle perhaps
            because Chuck Connors in *The Rifleman* beat
him to the punch with an entire Winchester which
            stood for utter and complete manhood
while Steve's peculiar but adequate gun subconsciously
            endeared him to those of us who were also
peculiar but adequate.

            The Blob, as if anyone could forget, was about
a ton of cranky Jell-O that oozed through town and
            absorbed people. It is one of those monsters that never
really caught on: think of a big Halloween party
            with a pack of Wolfmen, a murder of Draculas,
more Frankensteins than you can shake a flaming stick
            at, but not one Blob.

In the film, half a dozen greasers and their hot rods
            are pitted against the local police,
but of course these same kids turn out to be the good
            lads who speed to their old high school
to fetch the CO2 fire extinguishers, because the Blob
            hated getting cold.

What interests me about this film, though, is not
        the predictable conflict or even Steve's girlfriend,
the homeliest love-interest since Flipper, but the city
        under attack from the Blob. It was called
Downingtown. Steve and some others are trapped
        by the Blob in the Downingtown Diner
and even when I first saw the film in 1958 all I could
        think of was the motto: Eat at the Downingtown
Diner Located Conveniently in Downtown Downingtown
        How big would the matchbook have to be?

One more thing: flash-frozen by the Army, the Blob was
        quickly flown to the Arctic where
it would more or less hibernate forever. Well, when
        Steve McQueen was dying of cancer,
he went to Juarez to have the local quacks freeze
        his tumors.

Lying beneath those foreign sheets he must have thought
        that he could emerge from this as he had
from the basement of the Downingtown Diner—
        shaken but ready for the next great escape
or motorcycle race because he was, let's face it,
        Steve McQueen.

Where I Live

There are lots of front porches and padded swings,
dozens of signs (purchased locally) that announce
This Way To Grandpa's Garden.

Local dogs are sleek and well-fed and if they
are watching anything, it is each other since
violence and crime are somewhere else, beating
up the timid and taking their lunch money.

The girl with the pin in her tongue who dispenses
coffee is friendly and goes to mass. The boy
with the tattoos really can fix anything and works
two jobs to support his ailing mother.

The Neighborhood Watch signs feature a cloaked
figure in a black hat, but I am sure if this fiend
should ever materialize he would be drawn to
an open window where Shirley Yamanaka plays

"Spring Song." Invited inside he would eat bread
and drink wine, too, and perhaps smoke a cigar.
On the patio. Not for him the pursuit by cudgel-bearing

villagers, but a new life in green slacks and polo
shirt, cronies in the Booster's Club, a place on
the sidelines as his step-daughter loops a foul ball
which he picks up and tosses back with spotless hands
that were once capable of anything.

Smoke

It seems like every day I come to
a crossroads. It's usually getting dark
and the weather-beaten arrows point
to places like the Ozarks or Transylvania.

I gather my cloak around me and wait.
In the morning I see that one road leads
to a pasture, another ends at a brook.

So I choose a dim path that winds through
the forest. To my dismay, no wolves.
Nothing but a whitewashed church,
a cozy inn, the inevitable daughter.

Let's say I stopped for awhile, met
those cerulean eyes, even distinguished
myself when the bandits rode in.

Eventually I'd leave the same note
on another polished table:

Gone for cigarettes